Savvy Surfing on the Internet

Searching and Evaluating Web Sites

Ray Spangenburg and Kit Moser

Enslow Publishers, Inc.

40 Industrial Road   PO Box 38
Box 398   Aldershot
Berkeley Heights, NJ 07922   Hants GU12 6BP
USA   UK

http://www.enslow.com

Dedication:
To Bob Steiner and Robert Sheaffer, heroic knights in the battle
against the dragons of unreason—
who also manage to make it fun along the way

Library of Congress Cataloging-in-Publication Data

Spangenburg, Ray, 1939-
     Savvy surfing on the Internet : searching and evaluating Web sites / Ray
Spangenburg and Kit Moser.
     p. cm. — (Issues in focus)
  Includes bibliographical references and index.
  ISBN 0-7660-1590-4 (hardcover)
  1. World Wide Web—Juvenile literature. 2. Browsers (Computer
programs)—Juvenile literature. [1. World Wide Web. 2. Internet.]
I.Moser, Diane, 1944- II. Title. III. Issues in focus (Hillside, N.J.)
TK5105.888 .S684   2001
025.04—dc21

                                         00-012655

Printed in the United States of America

10 9 8 7 6 5 4 3 2

To Our Readers: We have done our best to make sure all Internet addresses in this
book were active and appropriate when we went to press. However, the author and
the publisher have no control over and assume no liability for the material available
on those Internet sites or on other Web sites they make link to. Any comments or
suggestions can be sent by e-mail to comments@enslow.com or to the address on the
back cover.

Trademarks: Most computer and software brand names have trademarks or registered
trademarks. The individual trademarks have not been listed here.

Illustration Credits: Click Art, p. 29; © Corel, pp. 8, 14, 18, 23, 60, 64,
83, 88, 96; © Corel Gallery, pp. 11, 35; © Dover Publications, p. 52;
Enslow Publishers, Inc., p. 74; Google Web site, p. 27; Library of Congress,
p. 62; Courtesy of NASA/JPL/Caltech, p. 69; "Netscape Communicator
browser window © 1999 Netscape Communications Corporation. Used with
permission. Netscape Communications has not authorized, sponsored,
endorsed, or approved this publication and is not responsible for its content,
p. 33; Ray Spangenburg and Kit Moser, pp. 16, 39, 56; Web site, p. 53.

Cover Illustration: © Mendola/Doug Chezem/The Stock Market.

Contents

Acknowledgments

A special thank you to everyone who spent time talking with us about their Internet experiences, both pleasant and disastrous, including Gary, Kit, Marta, Amber, Ryan, Eric, David, Diane, and Darrell. And kudos to Teresa Lum, our HTML wizard.

Introduction

Say "Internet," and most people think "high-tech" power, speed, and glitz. They may also think of keeping in touch with friends through e-mail and Web pages, or chatting online. They also usually think of wide-open access to information—lots and lots of different kinds of information. The Internet is both useful and "with it." It can be both amusing and thought provoking. The Internet lets you travel down many roads you might not otherwise come across. That is both the good news and the bad news.

The Internet's excitement and beauty is ours to appreciate and enjoy. Like any deep and powerful waters, the Internet can transport its users to every imaginable kind of destination. It is up to us, the users, to determine what destinations we want to visit and, perhaps most important of all, how we decide to use what we find.

The Internet began around 1974, before personal computers, when scientists found they needed a quick and easy way to keep in touch with the work other scientists were doing. Engineers—especially those working on military or space contracts—also needed a way to keep up with progress in their fields. They used computer modems to obtain updates on specialized information by dialing in to specialized electronic information centers—or databases. Many such databases and exchange centers existed, but the general public did not have access to them. Links were made directly among university computers, huge computer systems at government agencies, and scientific laboratories, and that was how the Internet first began.

Today, the Internet is a very different place. Now, many more sites exist and most are open to the public. It has been described as a vast "commercial playground."[1] It can be a lot of fun—full of photographs, cartoons, games, music, and even animations. It is also a great research tool for everyone—from students to dentists, from investors to librarians, from children to parents. Scientists and government agencies still use Internet connections, of course, and most ordinary people still do not have access to their discussions and databases. However, anyone can look up the holdings of the Library of Congress. Any user can check news stories on dozens of online newspapers—and get views on the same story from many different regions. How does the story look from London? Check *The London Times*. See how it is handled on the urban East Coast by checking *The New York Times*. Travel through cyberspace to the western United States by reading *The Portland Oregonian*. People can read magazine articles, see museum exhibits, and explore specialized sites about arts and sciences. The National Park Service offers information on the Web about every national park. The town of Salmon, Idaho—a remote village isolated in the wilderness regions of the Salmon National Forest—displays beautiful pictures of the region on its Web site. Just a few years ago people had to travel many miles, write letters and wait weeks or subscribe to magazines or visit libraries to obtain this kind of information.

Yet commercialism—an emphasis on sales, business, and profit—is extremely common on the Internet. Propaganda, hoaxes, and incorrect information abound on the Internet. That is why the Internet is a good place to find information, but only if you are careful, as librarian John R. Henderson says.[2] Other experts agree. The only sure defense against getting fooled is constant skepticism.

Whew! Skepticism? Lots of people think skepticism is a really negative word. It seems to imply lack of trust, maybe even a suspicious attitude. But being skeptical does not mean not believing anything. It just means asking questions (and seeking answers) about everything. It is definitely a lot better than being fooled.

"Doubt is the beginning of wisdom," goes the proverb.[3] When surfing the Internet, doubt is not only the beginning of wisdom. It may also mean the difference between knowing and being fooled.

This book is about that difference. To begin, take a look at a tall tale that passed for real on the Internet—the tale of a banana-borne bacteria that eats people alive.

Who would think that as harmless and healthy an object as a banana would cause widespread panic? An e-mail describing a "flesh-eating banana" led to just such a panic for several weeks, until it was established that the communication had been a hoax.

The Great Flesh-Eating Banana Hoax

In early January 2000, many thousands of people found the following warning among their e-mail messages on their computers:

Bad Bananas

Warning:

Several shipments of bananas from Costa Rica have been infected with necrotizing fasciitis, otherwise known as flesh eating bacteria.

Recently this disease has decimated the monkey population in Costa Rica. We are now just learning that the disease has been able to graft

9

itself to the skin of fruits in the region, most notably the Banana which is Costa Rica's largest export. Until this finding scientist were not sure how the infection was being transmitted. It is advised not to purchase Bananas for the next three weeks as this is the period of time for which bananas that have been shipped to the US with the possibility of carrying this disease.

If you have eaten a banana in the last 2-3 days and come down with a fever followed by a skin infection seek MEDICAL ATTENTION!!! The skin infection from necrotizing fasciitis is very painful and eats two to three centimeters of flesh per hour. Amputation is likely, death is possible. If you are more than an hour from a medical center burning the flesh ahead of the infected area is advised to help slow the spread of the infection. The FDA has been reluctant to issue a country wide warning because of fear of a nationwide panic. They have secretly admitted that they feel upwards of 15,000 Americans will be affected by this but that these are "acceptable numbers". Please forward this to as many of the people you care about as possible as we do not feel 15,000 people is an acceptable number.

Manheim Research Institute[1]

Unbelievable—And Untrue, Too

Thousands of people received this dramatic e-mail on their computers during the first weeks of 2000—and it scared a lot of them. It sounded real and frightening. Many people took it seriously, or at least thought it *might* be true and sent the warning along to their friends. Lots of people gave up eating bananas for

Though e-mail most frequently contains messages from friends, it is also a favorite dumping ground for those circulating hoaxes and urban legends.

awhile. The fright they went through was needless, though, because the e-mail was not true. Investigators soon verified that it had no foundation in fact. (Fortunately, no reports came in about anyone burning away portions of their skin.)

The "Flesh-Eating Bananas" e-mail (as it came to be called) is just one of thousands of hoaxes and urban legends that circulate throughout the Internet every day. These untrue stories may arrive as e-mail, or people may come across them on Web sites. They come up in chat room conversations and newsgroups, or someone might just tell about "the weird thing I found on the Net today."

Webster's College Dictionary defines a hoax as: "1. Something intended to deceive or defraud. 2. To deceive by a hoax; hoodwink."[2] A hoax is a story intentionally made up by someone to fool people.

An urban legend is an unverified story handed on as true. Urban legends often develop variations and additional details as they are passed from one person to another. They also usually reflect the influence of the communities they grow in. Jan Harold Brunvand is an American folklorist who has written several books about urban legends, including *Curses! Broiled Again!: The Hottest Urban Legends Going.* In that book he describes urban legends as "those bizarre but believable stories about batter-fried rats, spiders in hairdos, Cabbage Patch dolls that get funerals, and the like that pass by word of mouth as being the gospel truth. Except they aren't true—they are contemporary folklore."[3]

So what is folklore? Turning again to *Webster's*, we find: "1. The traditional beliefs, legends, customs, etc., of a people; lore of a people. 2. The study of such lore. 3. A body of widely held but false or unsubstantiated beliefs."[4]

It is definition 3 that is of interest here: "A body of widely held but false or unsubstantiated beliefs." So, in Brunvand's definition, when he talks about contemporary folklore, he means simply those stories and beliefs that we create, tell, read about, or listen to, *today*. Traditional folklore may spin tales of Paul Bunyan and Babe, his blue ox, or headless horsemen and phantom trolls. But contemporary folklore, or urban legends, are more likely to be wild yarns about life today—a story about a neighbor's pet Doberman pinscher dog running around with an intruder's detached hand in his mouth, or a tale about human beings being kidnapped by flying saucers.

Urban legends are great stories. Sometimes they are scary, sometimes funny. Sometimes they even try to teach us something. Sometimes we believe them, and sometimes we do not. They are part of our culture. Sometimes they tell us a lot about who we are and what we think or feel about things—but most of the time they never really happened.

It is often hard to tell where and when urban legends start. Folklorists spend a lot of time trying to track them back to their beginnings. Sometimes they are lucky and they can get pretty close; usually, though, pretty close is as close as they get.

Most experts now think the flesh-eating bananas story started out as a hoax. (There is such a disease as necrotizing fasciitis, but it is very rare, is generally not carried by food, and the bacteria that cause it would not survive long on a banana.[5]) Someone, somewhere, made up the story, probably thinking that it would be a pretty good joke. Or, some people suggest, the original yarn spinner may have stood to gain if people stopped eating Costa Rican bananas. Maybe the originator was a competing banana grower, for example. The original storyteller either posted the story directly on the Internet or told it to someone else, who probably believed it and passed it on. Then it kept getting passed on by word of mouth

Sometimes real life and urban legend overlap. In 2001, a dog in San Francisco killed an apartment dweller. In cyberspace legend, a Doberman ran around with a neighbor's hand gripped in his mouth.

until someone along the line sent out the original e-mailed warning. People who received it sent it on to their friends, and it was copied and re-posted over and over again until literally thousands of these e-mail warnings flooded the Internet. (E-mail software makes this process easy, and many users have lists of addresses to which they like to forward funny stories, jokes, and chain letters they have received. It is as simple as selecting the received message, clicking on a group of addresses in the software's "Address Book," and clicking on the "Forward" button.) This is the life story of most e-mail hoaxes.

It is the amazing power of the Internet and its ability to reach so many people in so short a time that allowed the flesh-eating bananas story to spread so fast and so far. In a matter of days, it truly became an urban legend.

Cyberspace—Full of Gems and Fool's Gold

The Internet is a remarkable tool. Some people even talk about it as a "place"—"cyberspace"—where information, communication, art, and commerce are readily available to everyone. A touch of the keyboard, a flicker on the computer monitor, and a student can get answers to research questions for her history homework. Her brother can read about his favorite movies or television shows. They can also learn more about their hobbies, read magazines, talk to friends, or play games. Anyone can investigate the mysteries of the universe or find out what Leonardo DiCaprio's favorite food is. It is possible to "travel"

•••••• Some Internet Jargon ••••••

domain name	The first parts of a *URL* (see below), usually two or three codes separated by periods and appearing before the first single forward slash (/); designates a particular machine. Examples: mail.example.com or www.example.com
http	HyperText Transfer Protocol, the primary method used on the World Wide Web (WWW) for transferring *hypertext* (see below) files between machines on the Internet.
hyperlink (also: link)	Text that contains words or phrases ("links") that the reader can click on to obtain additional information or comment, either from another document or from another place in the same document.
hypertext	Any text that contains *hyperlinks*.
Internet (upper-case I)	(also called the Net) The huge, global interconnection of *networks* that use the protocol called *TCP/IP* (see below).
internet (lower-case i)	(as opposed to the *Internet*) A system of two or more networks connected together.
network	A system of two or more computers connected so that they can share resources, such as printers, modems, and drives.
TCP/IP	(Transmission Control Protocol/Internet Protocol) The group of protocols (standard regulating procedures for exchanging data between computers) used on the Internet.
top-level domain	The last code in a *domain name*, usually the most general of the designations, indicating a country of origin (such as .ca for Canada) or a type of site (such as .edu for an educational institution).
URL	(Uniform Resource Locator) The standard way to give an address that is located on the World Wide Web. Examples: http://www.anysource.com/special.html or news:new.newusers.questions
World Wide Web (WWW)	(World Wide Web) Technically, the group of servers that allows text, graphics, sound, and other files to be mixed together; the most widely used portion of the Internet.

In order to use the Internet effectively, it is helpful to learn its most common jargon.

thousands of miles to visit an art museum in Paris or London or listen to a rock concert from Moscow. The Internet offers just about anything anyone would want to know about the stars in the skies or the "stars" on movie screens. It has been called the greatest source of information in the history of the world—the Information Superhighway.

Like most highways, though, the Information Superhighway can be dangerous and requires some caution. The case of the great "Flesh-Eating Bananas" scare in January 2000 is not unusual. The information on the Information Superhighway is not always true. In fact, cyberspace is filled with bad information, misinformation, and outright lies. In the days of the California gold rush, people flocked to the hills to prospect for precious ore. Wealth was nearly free for the taking with a little hard work and a small stake of food and supplies. However, some people stumbled on a bright, shiny metal that seemed to be gold, but was worthless. It was actually a rock known to geologists as iron pyrites, but it soon earned the name "fool's gold." A lot of what people come across on the Internet may be more like fool's gold than the real thing.

Now that is a pretty scary thought. Suppose a student plans to jump onto the Net to find some facts for a history essay. Or maybe someone wants to search on the Internet to find out what might be wrong with a sick dog or cat—and find out how to treat it. Some of the information he or she finds may be true—and some may not be.

The Information Superhighway can be a great place to learn, but sorting out real information from the fake takes both know-how and caution.

How Can So Much Be So Wrong?

A lot of people have trouble accepting the idea that the Internet could contain incorrect information. Why would anyone give wrong information or lie? How would information get on the Internet if it is wrong?

It is not easy to answer the first question. Part of the answer is that human beings make mistakes, and the Internet is not just a vast superhighway of computers and Web sites. Behind every Web page are human beings—and everyone is capable of making honest mistakes. Some people may know more about a subject than others, but even experts make mistakes. Also, sometimes people pretend to be, or think that they are, experts when they are not.

Unfortunately, honest mistakes are only part of the story. Sometimes, for many reasons of their own, people deliberately lie. Three of the major reasons are:

1) They may want their readers to accept an idea of theirs, or a philosophy they hold.

2) They may want to sell a product.

3) They may want to collect e-mail addresses for future use—usually to contact readers with a sales pitch or a scam.

Let us take a quick look at each of these reasons. First, people may lie or exaggerate to convince or persuade—to "sell" all kinds of ideas. Some of those ideas may be ugly and destructive. Racists, cults, and other groups that promote hatred often distort facts and exaggerate to make a point. A Web page can, in fact, be created and placed online by anyone—even people who have criminal intentions. No central agency edits them. There is no Internet "traffic cop" to stop dishonest information from getting posted. Readers are on their own, and they may not have the usual cues to rely on to make judgments. They do not see the people who post Web pages, and they may not even know the name of the person who wrote what they read. (People with positive intentions also sometimes lie. They may think a little lie will not hurt anyone. They may even excuse their lies by thinking that good will come of them. However, they are still lies, and anyone who cares about what is true and what is not should watch out for this, too.)

Second, there is the mighty dollar. Some people will say anything to make money, and it is a case of "reader beware." Many e-mail scams make their rounds on the Internet. One woman reported that she received an e-mail announcing that she had won third prize in a travel contest. "All she had to do" was send ten dollars. Then she noticed the fine print: An additional ninety-five dollars was required to seal the deal. Remember the old saying: "If it sounds too good to be true, it probably is."

Web pages promote products that claim to cure all kinds of illnesses—and many of these "cures" are incapable of curing anything. According to a representative of the U.S. Food and Drug Administration (FDA), "Of great concern to us at the FDA is the promotion of colloidal silver on the Internet, which is falsely claimed to provide cures for tuberculosis and the plague." She also mentioned promotion of a substitute for insulin (used to control diabetes). It turned out to be just distilled water combined with extremely small amounts of salt. The Internet is not the only place where people try to sell products that are not what they claim, but it is a low-cost, low-effort way of reaching customers. So, it is easy to encounter both honest and dishonest merchants there—and it is important to be able to tell the difference.

The third kind of "lying" is also hard to detect.

Most people who are selling something on the Internet make use of information they gather about visitors to their site. So, they will ask for e-mail addresses and other details—to reach these visitors in the future. These merchants or sites may offer prizes or gift certificates in exchange for information. This may not necessarily be dishonest—unless they hide what they are planning to do with the information. They may sell it or pass it on to other merchants, and soon they and their "business partners" are stuffing e-mail boxes with unwanted ads (known as "spam"). Giving information to strangers on the Web can be dangerous. Without a go-ahead from parents, a teacher, or another trustworthy adult, a good rule of thumb is "just say no."

Of course, people sometimes lie simply because they are out to create a hoax for mischief, "just for the fun of it." That is probably what happened in the story of the flesh-eating bananas.

How does information get on the Internet if it is wrong? That is the easy question to answer. It is important to remember that *anyone can put anything on the Internet.* Today, Web browsers (software for accessing the Internet) and software for creating Web pages are becoming both more sophisticated and easier to use. More and more people—from high school juniors to art students in college, from fifth graders to their moms and dads—are creating their own Web pages. All it takes is an Internet connection, the proper software, a little knowledge, a little patience, and a few hours. Almost anyone can create a Web page. One estimate of Web pages indexed on the

World Wide Web in October 2000 was well over one billion.[6] Think about the size of that number. And many more thousands of pages are added every day.

Not an Electronic Library

It is easy to see why many people think of the Internet as kind of a gigantic electronic library where they can find anything they want just by using a search engine. It is like hunting through a library's electronic catalog or card catalog. Look up "dogs," and thousands of sites on dogs may spring up on the screen. Look up "cats," and browse through a ton of information on cats. And the same is true of most subjects.

The difference, though, is that the public library's holdings represent a *selection* of material. The Internet can and does contain anything and everything. At the library, professionally trained people have carefully selected all the books and all the magazines on its shelves. Most of these books and magazines are published by professional publishers who have carefully edited them and have checked the facts. The authors and specialists who write these materials must meet the standards set for them by the book or magazine publishers. Some books or magazines are highly specialized or technical, such as science books, or books on medicine, history, or finances. In these cases, most publishers have had them read and reviewed by other experts in these fields before they are published. This process gives the author of the book or magazine article an opportunity to find and correct any mistakes, omissions, or errors before publication.

This process does not guarantee that everything in the library is true or error free, or even that it is well written or well thought out. But at least a reader can be reasonably sure that many people besides the author have carefully read the material and evaluated the value of its contents before it has found a place on the library shelves.

Now, take a look at the more than one billion pages that currently make up the portion of the Internet called the World Wide Web. The first thing

It is easy to get too much information too quickly from the Internet. As of 2000, there were one billion Web pages to scan.

to remember is that the World Wide Web is *not* a library, although it appears to have some things in common with a library. It is actually much more like an incredibly gigantic bulletin board. No single person or group oversees what may or may not be placed on it.

Many trustworthy organizations, publishers, corporations, associations, or groups of individuals do govern what appears on their particular Web sites. However, any single individual or group of individuals can, for a very little cost, create and post a Web page at any time with no responsibility to anyone. Anyone can speak his or her mind, as eloquently or awkwardly as he or she wishes, about any subject at all. Experts and amateurs can speak of stars and planets, of life and death, of dogs and cats. No one final authority edits or checks the material that turns up on the Internet.

This wonderful freewheeling, freethinking democracy of the Internet is the source of both its powers and its pitfalls. The Internet is unquestionably the greatest single source of information in the history of humankind. At no time in history has it been so easy to find the answers to so many questions so quickly and effortlessly.

The trick is to be able to tell the facts from the fictions, the truths from the lies, and the distinguished from the distorted—because all these forms can be found on the Internet in abundance. This book will explain how to develop the skills to think critically about what you see and what you read, so you can tell the difference.

Looking for Answers on the Internet

Two Internet experts, Steve Lawrence and C. Lee Giles from the NEC Research Institute, estimated in a 1999 study that during the year 2000 the Web would grow to over 2,200 million pages. That is a lot of pages and a lot of information available at our fingertips.[1]

Getting at all this information may seem as simple as jumping on a search engine, keying in a few words, and checking out the results. However, after taking a look at the pages and pages and pages of results, most people sigh with frustration. A good search takes more than just a few quick keystrokes.

A search engine is a computer program that usually uses a "spider" (sometimes called a "crawler" or a "bot") to crawl through the vast quantities of information on a large number of Web sites, looking for topics that someone somewhere might want to know about. Then the program creates a huge index, or catalog. Most people think that when they enter a search term in a search engine, their computer goes out to search the entire Internet in response to their request. Actually, though, the search engine's own computers have already done that, long before the first user typed in a request. Each search engine, using its own techniques, periodically roams the Internet and uses various methods to make an index of the information available. When an Internet user types in a search request, the search engine compares the words or phrases in the request to the entries in its index and displays the results—which can number in the hundreds of thousands.

One search engine claimed in July 2000 that it currently indexed more than one billion pages.[2] Still, a search engine cannot possibly cover everything on the Net. According to Lawrence and Giles,[3] only about one third of the estimated total of Web pages is covered by even the best search engines. The creators of search engines work hard at trying to keep up. They constantly develop new techniques for increased speed and coverage, but Lawrence and Giles predict that it will be another ten to twenty years before they even begin to catch up. If the Web were a giant iceberg, most of it would remain underwater while only the tip would be accessible. Still,

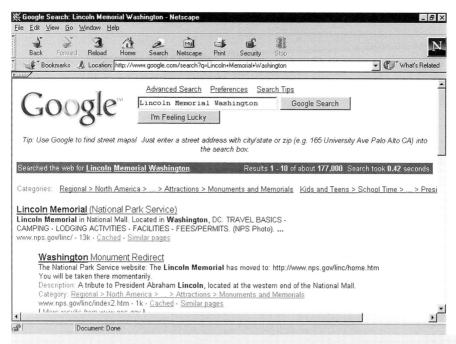

A search engine is something like a sifter or sorter—so that, when a person types in an information request, the results can come up quickly.

even that tip represents a lot of information. So much, in fact, that managing, understanding, and evaluating it all may become more than anyone—or any computer—can possibly do.

A recent search on one popular search engine using the words "alien abductions" turned up over 180,380 pages. How truthful or useful all that information might be is another matter altogether. (*See* Appendix: About "Alien Abductions.") It is a search engine's job to return all the information it can, based upon the query made to it. It does this through a variety of specialized techniques. In the competitive world of search engines, each one tries to do a better job at bringing in more and more "hits" faster and more efficiently than its competitors. It is not the search engine's job, though, to judge the truth or honesty of any of the information that it relays. The search engine's job is done when it delivers a long list of Web page addresses—known as *URL*s ("Uniform Resource Locators"). Sorting the truths from the fictions, the facts from the fantasies, the valid from the invalid, is the reader's job—and in the wide, often weird world of the Web, sometimes that is an incredibly tough job.

Do Not Get Taken

So, things are often not what they seem. However, by looking past the obvious for clues—as Sherlock Holmes might do—the savvy user can usually uncover the truth. This practice can be as challenging as a chess game—and it can also be both fun and enlightening. Seeing past a sham or spoof and spotting the truth can be a lot more interesting—and sometimes a lot less dangerous—than believing someone's hyped-up advertising or fantastic story.

One of the sites turned up in the search for "alien abductions" was a clever spoof designed to look like the official page of a so-called UFO "contactee" organization. Organizations like these usually promote first-person stories from people who claim that aliens kidnapped them and took them aboard flying saucers. The storytellers are often emotional,

A person can get plenty of information on the Web, but to figure out whether the information is accurate and honest, one has to look for clues, as Sherlock Holmes used to do.

even hysterical, and neither the Web site nor the storytellers question the stories. However, this page was different. It offered to use hypnosis and various other means to convince anyone who desired the service that they, too, had been among the fortunate elite who had been abducted by the little green men. Continuing its spoof, the site also offered low-cost courses in deprogramming, medication, and therapy to anyone who had availed themselves of the alien abduction service, so that they could discontinue the fake experience they had paid for in the first place.

Unfortunately, though, while this UFO site was a clever spoof, easily seen through by just about anyone, the alien abductions search also turned up many handsomely designed, official-looking, and authentic-sounding sites that promoted uncritical acceptance of even the most outlandish claims of alien abduction. Of the first twenty-five sites offered by one popular search engine, twenty-three were obvious promotions for this unfounded claim, while only two offered any kind of balanced approach to the subject.

Clearly, in the search for useful and truthful information, navigating the World Wide Web can be both frustrating and misleading.

Search Engine Turnover

The 1999 Lawrence and Giles study showed that 85 percent of all the people who use the World Wide Web use search engines to help them find the information they are looking for.[4] Despite their limitations, search engines are the most effective way to locate information on the Web. There are some simple facts about search engines that are useful to keep in mind, though. The first is that like everything else on the Web, search engines keep changing. Programmers love to tinker and corporations love to devour one another. This month's hot search engine may be next month's fizzle as it transforms from early to later versions, or changes hands from one developer to another. More than one "leading edge" search engine has failed to keep up its steam in the competitive world. Soon it resembles all the rest in only a few months' time.

The Nature of the Search

When we ask a search engine to find "alien abductions," for instance, it searches its own computers to provide a list of all the sites that it has previously found that seem to match our request in one way or another. The key phrase here is "seem to," since each search engine uses unique methods to look for and sort out the information that it has gathered in its periodic Internet roaming. Also, programmers have set up each particular search engine to present information according to unique standards. These standards are used to determine the relevance and order of presentation for its results. So, each search engine has its own personality and unique way of thinking. However, like people, search engine personalities change. Because developers and programmers continually try to keep up with changes in what is available and what people want, they try out new techniques and sometimes make major changes in their search methods. So, search engines are in a constant state of evolution.

Also, people who develop Web sites are keenly aware of the importance of search engines for Internet users. Commercial sites want all the traffic they can get in order to sell their products or advertising. Nonprofit and personal pages also want all the "visitors" they can get. Many home pages sport a proud announcement that "xxx" number of visitors have viewed this site since such and such a date. Newspapers reported that a NASA page covering the activities of a robot spacecraft on the surface of Mars received over 265 million hits in a single day.

So, some Web page designers have figured out ways to trick search engines into listing their pages more prominently than really makes sense. That is, the page does not really contain the popular information the search engine thinks it has found. For example, Web designers sometimes pack a Web page with a number of relevant key words that a search engine might be looking for, even though the main subject of the page may be much more limited in scope. For example, a search for information on epilepsy might turn up several commercial pharmaceutical sites before listing a site for the Epilepsy Foundation, which would probably have much less biased information. The authors created the Web site to provide objective information, not to sell medications for epilepsy.

The best rule of thumb for using search engines is: Never rely on only one. A good researcher or news reporter would never use only one source of information. So, why rely on only one source to find out where that information can be found? Because each one works slightly differently, each will give different results.

People often have a favorite search engine that appears to work well for their purposes. But it is always a good idea to back it up by using a couple of others—and to change the backup engines occasionally. Search engine technology is still in its infancy.

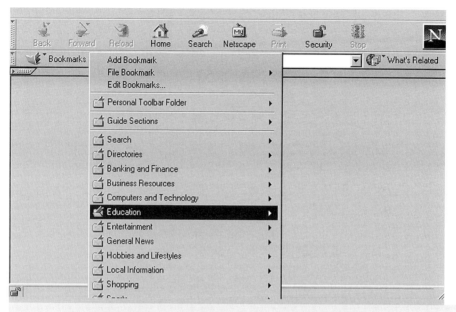

When a good site or search engine is found, it is a good idea to mark it as a favorite ("bookmark" it) for future use.

New search engines are always coming online and older ones are constantly disappearing.

Another approach that works well is to use one search engine to look for others, or even look for pages that have hyperlinks to many other search engines. It is a good trick to find and bookmark a couple of those pages. (Look on the Menu bar of your browser—the software you use to surf the Net. Find the Favorites or Bookmarks choice—possibly under another menu item, such as Communicator. Then just click on "Add to Favorites" or "Add to Bookmarks" when you have a page open that you want to return to often.) Another tip: Create a folder called "Search" in the "Favorites" or "Bookmarks" menu option of the Web browser and add favorite search engine sites there. This method will keep favorite search engines handy for whenever they are needed.

Play Detective—Dig Deeper

Sleuthing out more details can be fun, and the deeper one digs the more interesting it gets. To learn something about snails, for instance, do not just stop at the first site that seems to have interesting snail information on it. Journalists have a good fact-finding guideline they call the "Rule of Three." That is, always use at least three sources. When reading a story in a newspaper, do not check just one newspaper online—read the story in two, three, or several different newspapers. (This is one of the great things about the Net—using multiple sources is easy.) Sometimes different papers will report the story a little differently, again giving the reader either more information or a slightly different understanding of that information.

What if the search engine turns up contradictory information? (It often will.) Keep looking and try to resolve the problem. Evaluate sources. *The New York Times*, for example, employs professional journalists and fact checkers to verify the articles it publishes, both online and in its newspaper. This certainly provides more reliable information than would usually appear on "Howie's Home Page," created by even the smartest sixth grader. Also, critical thinking skills need to be applied.

Be a detective. If you read information saying that snails love quails, look at other information sites to verify or deny.

Better Than a Search Engine?

For all their shortcomings, search engines take users to places they would never have thought of looking—providing exciting access to information resources all over the world. However, when the accuracy of information really matters, some experts prefer the surer, quicker method of working from a list of URLs recommended by sources that are knowledgeable about the research topic.

In an Internet article written in June 2000, Dr. David Biro, a dermatologist, recounted a test he made with the topic "acne." He typed the topic into the search field of a popular search engine, clicked on "Go" and waited for the answers to roll in. More than one hundred suggested sources did pop up on Biro's computer screen. However, he writes, "Of the first 10 entries, . . . seven were useless." Most were commercial sites selling pharmaceutical remedies or unrelated services and providing little or no information about acne. Biro concluded that, without a professional background in dermatology, most users would find it difficult to tell the sound information from advice offered to bolster a sales pitch for products that might or might not be useful.

Who would know more useful information about acne, its causes, and its possible cures? Dr. Biro suggests using either a targeted search engine (a searcher that specializes in this type of information) or going directly to one or more Web sites devoted exclusively to medical information. If you use a desktop computer at school or at the public library, you may find that librarians or teachers have set up preselected sites that can be extremely useful to students. (Using the "Rule of Three," taking a look at three or more sites would be a good idea for a broad, balanced understanding.) Biro suggests government-supported, broad-based sites such as the National Library of Medicine, as well as some commercial sites that offer general health information. For specific health problems, he also suggests finding sites that offer information that relates directly to those ailments.[5] For example, the American Academy of Dermatology's Web page would offer balanced information about acne and other skin diseases.[6]

Finally, remember that not everything is on the Internet. Most material written before the 1980s is not available on the Internet—and that is a lot of material![7] Do not be afraid to close down the computer and go to sources that are not on the Internet. There are many other ways and places to get information. When a question comes up—whether the project is a paper to be written, a quick question to answer, or a problem to be solved—ask yourself whether the Internet is the best place to find the information that is needed. Could you flip a few pages of a dictionary to find the definition you need? Or is the word you are looking for more easily found on the Internet because it is too recent or technical (a word such as hypertext or URL, for example) to be found in your five-year-old dictionary? Finding some answers can be done faster and more accurately by just opening a reference book and flipping a few pages. It is easy to spend an hour on the Internet looking for a piece of information that could have been found in five minutes or less offline. A good researcher and balanced thinker keeps all his or her options open.

3

Would You Believe: "I WAS A VICTUM OF SPACE CRETURES!!!"

The Web page illustration "I WAS A VICTUM OF SPACE CRETURES!!!" is imaginary, but it is not too different from a lot of pages found on the Web. It is easy to see mistakes right in the title, and not many people would take it seriously. Unfortunately, though, some would—especially if it is decked out with some nifty graphics, Java applets, or colorful animations.

Jazzy graphics are fun, but when a person is looking for solid information—reliable answers to count on—graphics are just window dressing. While the window dressing may be cool, if a reader is looking for facts or good advice and the text is not reliable, he or she comes away empty-handed. Or, even worse, a person might think he has found reliable information when all he has found is misinformation, lies, or just plain nonsense.

Even though it is easy to see through the example story, "I WAS A VICTUM OF SPACE CRETURES!!!" this Web page gives us a good chance to notice a few

I WAS A VICTUM OF SPACE CRETURES!!!

Eyewitness Stories:

Kidnapped by Aliens!!

Your source for information about Alien Abductions!

"I am a rocket engenear working for NASA and like most people I didn't believe in flying saucers. But something happend to me that convinced me that they were real!!!! TODAY I AM A BELIEVER! I have decided to tell this story because there are many people in the world who are sceptics like I was once, and I now believe that this scepticsism is VERY DANGEROUS!!!

I now know that UFOs ARE REAL!! and the United States goverment is trying to keep the TRUTH from us!! I WAS CAPTURED AND HELD PRISONER by a flying saucer!!! And I now know the terribal things that are in store for us if we fail to believe in this menice! The World is in for a DEVASTATING DISASTER if we do not pay attention. The Aliens told me about their SECRET PLANS for the destruction of our earth and about the amazing technoligy that they have developed to help them in there cruel endevor! Even though I am a trained physisist I was ASTOUNDED by the AMAZING LEVEL OF THERE SCIENCE AND TECHNOLIGY!

While I was held prisoner I was SUBJECTED TO TREMENDOUS CRUELTY on the part of my capters and I was told that they are not like us. That THEY DO NOT HAVE FEELINGS!! THEY DO NOT HAVE EMOTIONS! One of my capters even told me that they would be very happy to SEE THE EARTH DESTROYED AND ALL OF IT'S INHABITENTS VANISHED FOREVER from the face of the universe!!!

The United States goverment is trying to stop me from telling this story. But I believe IT MUST BE TOLD!!

Web pages that are not valid sources of information usually give out signs such as obvious misspellings that show a careful (or even not so careful) reader that the site is not serious.

red flags—typical signals to use for recognizing a Web page that may not be trustworthy.

Bad Spelling

A document containing lots of spelling mistakes, improper punctuation, or grammatical errors says something about the creator: It is a warning sign that not a lot of care has gone into the site. Everyone makes mistakes in spelling at one time or another. That is why word processing programs have spellcheckers. And certainly if someone makes a spelling mistake, that does not necessarily mean that he or she is not trustworthy. But take a closer look at "I WAS A VICTUM OF SPACE CRETURES!!!"

The writer is claiming to be a highly educated person, a rocket engineer. He or she made this claim to establish authority—as a well-educated professional who is able to report accurately. Training as a rocket engineer requires discipline and intelligence, so many readers would trust a person with this background.

However, the story told is a little outside a rocket engineer's professional area of qualification. A wise skeptic might well ask what rocket engineering has to do with being victimized by aliens from space.

However, the biggest, brightest flashing warning sign in this Web page is its bad spelling. Now we find ourselves asking some very specific questions. Would a real rocket engineer not know how to spell engineer? Or technology? Could a "trained physisist" who cannot even spell the word "physicist" really get anything off the ground? Readers may find themselves wondering about this writer's claim. Maybe the writer is not really a rocket engineer. In fact, that possibility looks very probable. And if that claim is not believable, why would anyone believe anything else the writer says?

OK, so this writer has been caught in a hoax. Or maybe the writer just intended to tell an entertaining story. However, what if the storyteller had not made the claim that he or she was a well-educated profes-sional? Perhaps the spelling errors are the oversights of a poorly educated but honest victim who had a story to tell?

That brings us to the biggest signal of all that bad spelling sends: If this person were really serious and wanted to be taken seriously, would not he or she at least have taken the time to use a good spellchecker? Or to ask a good speller to look it over? Remember, in most cases, if you can find something on the Internet, anyone else in the world can view it, too. And when posting an article on the Web for the world to see, most people would take a little care with any-thing they wanted taken seriously.

The writer of this story apparently did not even have the sense to know that he or she was a bad speller and did not know it mattered. That is a pretty basic lack of good sense.

Lots of "Caps" and "Bangs"

Like bad spelling, an excess of uppercase letters ("caps") and exclamation marks ("bangs") does not necessarily mean that the writer cannot be trusted. However, those "caps" and "bangs" do send up a red flag. Most serious documents can stand on their content alone. They do not need to call attention to themselves by typographical exaggeration. Even more than one exclamation at the end of a sentence is tabloid-style writing—found in one of the sensational newspapers (tabloids) often on display at supermarket checkout stands. It is the sort of punctuation that often turns up in an extra-bold tabloid headline such as, "Man Has 120-Pound Tumor and Doesn't Even Know It!!!" The tabloid newspapers use this style to get readers excited or to gain attention for unbelievable and untrue information disguised as facts. Tabloids are famous for overstatements, runaway exaggeration, and outright hoaxes. When writers use tabloid style, they send out a warning signal that they are trying to manipulate their readers in the same way.

Try counting the number of exclamation points in the sample story. Also, how many words are all uppercase letters? This typographical style signals that the writer is either exaggerating on purpose or is naive. Either way, the reader cannot be sure the "facts" are right.

Overly Emotional Writing Style

Is the writer letting his or her emotions run wild? Are the statements extravagant? Is the writing overly enthusiastic and does it attempt to manipulate people's emotions?

Emotion is a powerful persuader, and many writers use an emotional style to capitalize on the reader's responses. This is certainly acceptable in a work of fiction, but if the document is claiming to be a factual account, then it is important to sort out the emotional content from the solid, verifiable facts.

The writer of "I Was a Victum of Space Cretures!!!" warns readers, "I now know the terribal things that are in store for us if we fail to believe in this menice! The World is in for a DEVASTATING DISASTER if we do not pay attention." These two sentences are full of emotion-packed words. Word choices such as "terrible," "menace," "devastating," and "disaster," all pile one on top of the other to raise near panic in the reader. Not even horror writer Stephen King—intent upon artfully scaring us—would pile that many warnings of impending doom in two little sentences.

When looking at an article that gives warnings like this, a reader is wise to give it some thought before letting it set her heart pounding. This much emotional language signals that the writer is trying to persuade—by jumping past the reader's brain and grabbing his emotions. It is a trick many people try to play, but going along with it without thinking can set the reader up for a whole range of pitfalls.

So, here is a tip: Look first to see if the writer supports the alarm with facts and logic. Are there verifiable facts and is the logic sound? Also, what is the writer's motive for all this emotional manipulation?

Faulty Logic

Problems with logic may not always be so obvious, but sometimes they are. Always read carefully. In the imaginary example above, the writer states that the aliens ". . . do not have feelings. They do not have emotions." And yet the writer later says, "one of my capters even told me that they would be very happy to see the Earth destroyed." If an alien does not have any emotions how can it then also be "very happy"?

Personal Anecdotes

When people tell a story about themselves—a personal anecdote—sometimes the tale is not really objective. That is, we tend to color a story we star in with our own emotions, ambitions, and wishful thinking.

Stories people tell about themselves can certainly be useful, and may even be truthful. But they should always be viewed cautiously. The simple fact is that people do not always tell the truth. Sometimes this is intentional and sometimes it is accidental. Humans, after all, are only human. Sometimes they can make honest errors in recounting events that they thought they remembered correctly. Sometimes their original perceptions or observations of an event were incorrect or biased. Sometimes, they embellish their stories or accounts in order to make the telling more interesting. In any case, such stories represent just one person's experience.

The Web can make personal anecdotes appear to have more authority than they really have.

Sometimes people think that if something is on the Internet—if they see it on their computer screen—then it must be true. Try asking this question: If someone came up to me at a bus stop and started telling me this story, would I believe him?

The "Wow! That is Fantastic!" Button

Not everything that sounds fantastic really is. Certainly, if a person had claimed five hundred years ago that someday pictures were going to move and speak and fly into people's houses where they could be watched on a big box, people would probably have laughed. However, it is a good rule of thumb to take a skeptical view of all fantastic-sounding stories or claims.

Remembering to be skeptical does not mean disbelieving everything—it just means giving oneself the right to question everything. The "farther out" a story is, the tougher the questions should be. Suppose someone tells a story or makes a claim that appears to contradict everything that most reasonably intelligent people hold to be true in the world. Then, the farther out the story is, the more it is up to the person telling the story or making the claim to prove that his or her story or claim is true.

For example, maybe a friend tells you he needs to borrow some money to feed the fifteen-thousand-pound, green, fire-breathing elephant that wandered into his garden last night. Do you believe that story? The burden of proof rests on the person making the claim. His story *may* be true, and if so, it would be exciting. But otherwise, it remains only an unproven story that deserves skepticism. Before you fork over the money your friend requests, you would probably want to see the fifteen-thousand-pound, green, fire-breathing elephant.

Unquestioning belief in UFOs and aliens who kidnap human beings may seem exciting—but playing detective and asking tough questions can actually be much more exciting. Also, if the stories or claims should turn out to be true, then the detective approach actually might help establish their truthfulness with solid facts and evidence.

Of course, often no opportunity arises for asking questions of the person who posts a fantastic story on a Web page. But think the questions anyway. Is there anything on the page that solidly establishes the truth of what the writer is claiming? Is there any way that it can be independently verified? Or, is the writer simply telling a story, offering no proof, and asking people just to believe the story because the person said it was true. If this is the case, it is probably time to move on because anyone with a little imagination can make up a good story.

If the author of the Web page claims to offer proof, continue to ask the tough questions. How legitimate is this "proof"? Does the creator of the Web page claim to have an object taken from the alien spaceship? Is it composed of a material unknown on Earth? Is a statement like this really proof? Does he or she really have it? Has the material been tested by experts to determine its actual composition? Who were these experts? Were they independent and unbiased? Are their reports available?

Also, the Web page may quote other people who claim to verify what the writer has said. Or it may provide links to other pages where still other people say they believe this writer's story. However, unless they can offer some kind of independent proof, or evidence of the truthfulness of the author's story, this is also just anecdotal evidence. That is, these people are just offering more stories in support of the original story. And a story is just that, a story—an anecdote offered as evidence or proof. Why should people believe these supporters any more readily than they believe the original author? Ten people can tell fibs just as easily as one can, especially if all ten people have a common interest in making people believe the story.

The next few chapters will examine some of the reasons people may have for telling things that are exaggerated or untrue, and how you can protect yourself from being fooled by them.

4

Investigating the Sources

Research is the art of finding information that is solid, accurate, and useful—and searching for a topic on a search engine may be the first step, but it is only the first step. Searches often deliver sites in the first few listings that seem to miss the point. Sometimes this happens because the user designed the search poorly and the search engine "misunderstands." Sometimes it happens because the search engine site has financial reasons for putting some sites first. We have also already seen that nothing ensures that the listed pages contain accurate information.

It is up to the user to evaluate how relevant any site on the list may be to his or her needs. That judgment is where research comes in.

Searching Well

What are the best words to describe what you are looking for? The best way to begin is by giving some thought to the topic and how to describe it so the search engine "understands." Words that have more than one meaning can bring up many listings that have no connection with the topic being researched. Maybe a horse enthusiast would like to find out about the source of bay coloring in horses, so she types in "bay" as her search word. This search produced a list of completely irrelevant entries in the first ten results when "bay" was used to query one search engine: a page for the Tampa Bay Online NETwork, news about the Examiner Bay to Breakers race in San Francisco, a site for the San Francisco Bay traveler, information about the Monterey Bay Aquarium, the Web site of the *San Francisco Bay Guardian* newspaper, information about a watershed restoration program for Chesapeake Bay, an item on the Green Bay Packers football team, a Web site for California State University at Monterey Bay, and Tampa Bay area news. Nothing at all about horses.

However, the addition of just two more words to the query produced much more helpful leads. Instead of "bay," our researcher tried using the words "bay color horses" to query the same search engine. Eight out of the first ten results dealt with coat color in horses, and all of them mentioned the color bay. The very first site was sponsored by the University of Missouri Extension Division and answered the question, What is a bay-colored horse? Another provided a list of books (with links) on equine coat color. A third site provided an updated article by a faculty member at the University of California at Davis School of Veterinary Medicine. Even if this article's discussion may have been a bit technical, additional sites mapped out the genetics clearly and simply. Two words made a lot of difference in this search, and this experience is typical. For focused results, phrasing the search well makes a big contrast and saves a lot of time and frustration.

"And" and "Or"

Some search engines also offer another way to refine a search, the use of "and" and "or." These are the two most commonly used "Boolean operators" (named after the mathematician George Boole). They signal what relationship the engine should require between the two words. Using "and" between two words means: Find Web sites that contain both Word 1 and Word 2. Using "or" between two words means: Find Web sites that contain either Word 1 or Word 2.

To find out if a search engine uses "and" and "or" (and possibly other methods for refining a search), look for a link marked "Advanced Search" or "About Searches" or "Click here to learn more about searching on this search engine" or something like that. Clicking on this link is a good idea, anyway, since search engines do have differences in the way they process the words entered for a search. Some look for the first word first. Others start with the last word. So if one of the words in the entry is the most important, knowing which way the search engine works would make a difference.

Also, many search engines assume that an entry such as "Appaloosa mare" really means "Appaloosa and mare." That is, it means, "Look for every Web page that contains both the words 'Appaloosa' *and* 'mare,' but not necessarily side by side." Some search engines respond more accurately, though, if you type "and" between the two words, and some require a "+." Placing quotes around two or more words usually signals to the search engine that this phrase should appear exactly as typed in the search entry. With some search engines, using "or" between words lets the search engine know that any one of two or more words will produce good results. To get good results with any search engine, though, it is always a good idea to find out exactly how it works by reading the information on its "Advanced Search" or "How to Search" link. They do not all work exactly the same way.

Who Provided the Site?

With a list of leads in hand, the next step is to check out the Web pages. Take a look at the URL. What is the source? Does the site identify its sponsor at the top of the page?

Sometimes a search engine will link directly to a

Like Dorothy in The Wizard of Oz, *sometimes a computer user "lands" on a site, but the home page is not clear. That means the user cannot identify the site.*

page deep inside a Web site, and the source of the information may not be obvious. This makes the user feel a lot like Dorothy in the Land of Oz. It seems as if suddenly "this isn't Kansas anymore," but exactly what it is may not be clear. (This strange effect is caused by the way search engines work and is usually not the fault of the Web site developer.)

When this happens, sometimes it is possible to delete some of the URL, forcing the Internet browser to show the home page of the site. From the home page, the source of the information may become clear. In the "bay color horses" search example, one site appeared without much indication of the source on the page. The URL looked like this:

The first part of the URL—between "http://" and the next forward slash (/)—is usually the "home" page. In this case, this designation ends in ".edu/"— a distinction that is often associated with a university or other educational institution (though not always). It is possible to find out more by placing the mouse cursor at the end of the line (after ".htm") and then using the backspace to remove the end of the URL up to that first forward slash after ".edu" and then pressing ENTER. (These illustrations are drawn from examples of one computer format, and other browsers and formats may have a different appearance.)

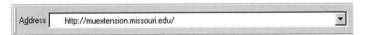

Once the new Web page comes up on the browser, it is easy to see that this is the Web site of the Extension Division of the University of Missouri at Columbia. The text on the page explains that the Cooperative Extension "includes operations that are part of the national Cooperative Extension System, a public educational network combining the resources of the U.S. Department of Agriculture, extension professionals at U.S. land-grant universities, county extension professionals and local governments." For anyone wanting more information about this program at the University of Missouri at Columbia, links are provided to additional pages describing the division's programs. Now the general source of the information on "Genetics of Coat Color of Horses" has become clear.

So, since this is information provided by a university, we can be certain it is correct, right? Wrong. Of course, it may be more likely to have reliable information than "Howie's Home Page." However, even when a site seems as reputable as this one, follow the Rule of Three. Find two other reputable sites, not linked to this one, and compare the information—just to be sure. Following the Rule of Three helps provide better understanding and sounder evidence in several ways.

- Comparison with other sources helps clear up any vague discussions by providing a different perspective.

- Use of different vocabulary and expanded detail increases understanding.

- Repetition of key facts may highlight the presence of typographical errors, misspellings, or misquoted statistics in other sources.

- On controversial topics, reading several different discussions can provide more balance and a more thorough exploration of the topic.

Who Created This Site and Why?

Web sites have different purposes. Who is the author of the site? A reputable site should not hide the identity of its author and should provide information about its purpose. Even if the author's credentials are not available, at least a means to contact him or her should be provided.

The domain name (the first parts of a site's URL, usually the first two or three parts, separated by periods and preceding the first single forward slash, /) may end in a code that can provide clues to the site's origin and purpose. This last entry, known as the top-level domain, is often one of three common codes: .com, .org, or .net. These three top-level domains originally indicated sites originating in the United States, but that is no longer strictly true. Generally, though, a site ending in .com is a commercial or for-profit site. The ending .gov indicates a site created and maintained by a government agency in the United States. The ending .org implies that a nonprofit organization, rather than a business, sponsors the site.

For example, http://www.un.org is a United Nations site. The URL for the Georgia O'Keeffe Museum is http://www.okeeffemuseum.org. Usually, these sites might be trusted at least not to have a profit motive behind their content. However, recently this distinction has become blurred, and today, some .org sites are actually commercial sites.

A Canadian government site usually ends in .ca, and sites originating in other countries typically (but not always) end in a two-letter code, such as .uk for United Kingdom and .jp for Japan. (See the chart "Some Domain Country Codes" for more country codes.)

Whenever a tilde (~) appears in a Web site

Some Domain Country Codes
•••••• (a partial list) ••••••

.am	Armenia	.et	Ethiopia
.ar	Argentina	.in	India
.as	American Samoa	.is	Israel
.at	Austria	.jp	Japan
.au	Australia	.kp	North Korea
.ba	Bosnia and Herzegovina	.kr	South Korea
.bi	Burundi	.mx	Mexico
.bm	Bermuda	.ne	Niger
.bo	Bolivia	.ng	Nigeria
.br	Brazil	.ni	Nicaragua
.ca	Canada	.nz	New Zealand
.cg	Congo	.pe	Peru
.ch	Switzerland	.ph	Philippines
.cl	Chile	.ru	Russian Federation
.cn	China	.sa	Saudi Arabia
.cu	Cuba	.to	Tonga
.de	Germany	.uk	United Kingdom
.dk	Denmark	.us	United States
.dz	Algeria	.za	South Africa
.eg	Egypt	.zw	Zimbabwe

Web site domains and e-mail from most nations usually end with two-letter abbreviations of the country's name, such as .uk for United Kingdom (sort of like our state names when we mail a letter).

address, it usually indicates that this is someone's personal Web page. The Internet computer connected with the domain name has provided space on its system for an individual's home page or Web site. This is often strictly a business arrangement (space provided for a fee) or a courtesy (space provided by a business for its employees or by a school for its students). The domain usually does not control anything, or much, about the Web page content. So, the tilde tips off users that this is a personal page.

However, the tilde tip-off does not turn up as often as in the past. Obtaining a domain for a personal site is no longer very expensive. (The user may still be using someone else's machine, but has paid for registration of his or her own domain name.) So instead of, say, http://www.myserver.com/~mypersonalsite (not a real URL), now something like http://www.mypersonalsite.com (also not a real URL) may appear instead. If the individual has chosen a commercial-sounding name, it may not be obvious right away that this site is maintained by an individual. It may have good information, too, but most individuals do not hire fact checkers and editors to verify the material they put on their personal Web pages. If they are careful and knowledgeable, they may provide excellent information. However, it is up to the user to figure out whether the Web site provides a resource that is good or bad, accurate or inaccurate. For anyone who is not an expert in the field discussed, that means finding an expert source and comparing the information. And even when looking at a site that seems to be trustworthy, compare its contents with other sites or sources—including books. (For example, it might be good to compare with a library book, an encyclopedia volume, or a CD-ROM encyclopedia.) Remember the Rule of Three.

The .edu URL

Teachers used to advise that a domain ending in .edu could be trusted. When the address contains .edu, the host site is usually attached to a school, college, or university. So, the conclusion was that its content was academically sound. However, today the .edu URL does not mean that everything accessed through that URL has the blessing of the school. Sites ending in .edu are associated with an educational institution. However, finding out exactly what the connection is may require a little more digging. Universities offer Web pages created and maintained by faculty members, who often know what they are talking about. Many schools allow students to develop Web pages on the school server, for example. Sometimes those pages are well thought out, and sometimes they are not. They may post unsubstantiated opinions and ideas, throw in poorly researched facts, or make available a brilliant, insightful paper on the history of the Huguenots. The problem is, there are no guarantees. So, do not put down your critical tools just because a domain name ends with .edu. It is important to evaluate this Web page's content with the same mixture of skepticism and enthusiasm as you would a site that has no academic connection.

The Link and Jump Hazard

One of the wonders of the Internet is its vast system of hyperlinks. While reading a topic, a user may stumble on something else of interest, click on the link, and find another path to follow, sometimes more fascinating than the first.

But hyperlinks can mean trouble. It is easy to leap from a reliable to a questionable site, without quite realizing it. While reading information on a site having knowledgeable authors, a user may follow a link to another site, completely unconnected with the first authors—a site that may or may not have the same reliability as the first one. In fact, the author may have provided the link to balance out his or her own point of view. That is fine, but then suppose the user follows links from the second site, getting further and further away from the original site. It is a good idea to pay close attention all along the way when following links, so that the source of the information is always clearly in mind.

Another hyperlink problem could be called the vicious circle of links: A source promoting a particular idea or concept usually offers links only to other sites that support the same viewpoint. So, it is easy to go from one to the other and then to another and another—and never get another perspective, unless you deliberately seek out a balance.

Follow the Money

Always ask this basic question: Who profits if readers accept what is said on this Web page? Especially

If a Web site praises the glories of a particular product, check to see whether that site is produced by a company that owns the product being promoted.

on commercial, for-profit Web sites this question comes up naturally. (As mentioned before, though, every site—not just the .com, or commercial site—has an agenda, something its owners want to accomplish.)

The difference between advertising, or promotion, and information is not always clear. Many Web sites that hope to sell products to their readers are designed to look like they are providing an informational service. It is surprising how many people are taken in by this ploy. They do not stop to think that a commercial Web site that sells shoes may not be an unbiased source of information about the health benefits of their magnetic insoles. Or that a Web page provided by a truck manufacturer will of course mention all the truck's glowing reviews in *U.S. Auto Driver*, the awards it has received, and the fact that millions were sold last year—but will never mention the low safety test ratings it received during unbiased consumer testing.

Can one also buy herbs from the Web site that claims to give objective opinions about how effective they are for curing ailments and making a person feel better? Better get another opinion from a Web site where the writers have less to gain if people believe them. What about the "trendsetting" clothes on a catalog page? Do these Web developers really know what they are talking about, or did they get stuck with a bunch of bell-bottom pants that are now out of style?

Hate Groups and Cults on the Internet

The First Amendment to the United States Constitution reads: "Congress shall make no law respecting an establishment of religion, or prohibiting the free exercise thereof; or abridging the freedom of speech, or of the press; or the right of the people peaceably to assemble, and to petition the Government for a redress of grievances."

Does this freedom mean that people have the right to display hate mottoes and propaganda on a Web site? Yes, it does. Freedom of speech is one of the most highly prized and important rights granted to United States citizens by the Constitution. Without

The First Amendment of the U. S. Constitution, contained in the Bill of Rights, allows for freedom of speech to all.

question, the most difficult test of our commitment to this right comes when we strongly disagree with the substance of what another citizen has to say. However, if we all agreed with each other, we would not need the protection of the First Amendment.

So, we cannot legislate hate and propaganda out of existence. Even if the First Amendment did not protect this right to free speech, no attempt to legislate it away would work. The only defense that works is to be perceptive, to notice hate propaganda when we see it, to be informed about it, and to educate others to watch for it, expose it, and counteract it wherever they see it.

Sometimes hatred flashes out at its readers in the form of burning crosses and swastikas. These symbols of hatred instantly tip off a surfer to the Web site's hateful intentions. However, hate propagandists are sometimes subtler than that. They may put forth brightly phrased, smoothly worded arguments. Their hatred may not be obvious on the surface. In that case, detecting their intentions is tougher and more challenging. Look for the logical fallacies discussed in the next chapter, and watch out for your own assumptions—they can trip you up.

Web sites provide a cheap means for spreading propaganda that can easily reach millions of readers, so hate groups and cults have hundreds of sites on the Internet. They may be visually attractive and technically sophisticated. The writing may be well phrased and may seem to be carefully reasoned. The top-level domain name may end in .org, .com, .net, or .edu. The site may originate in any country

Highly biased web pages may promote hate groups.

anywhere in the world. So, the first guideline for avoiding being taken in by hate group and cult propaganda is to critically examine everything on any Web site.

Watch foremost for three features that most hate sites—as well as hate-oriented newsgroups and chat rooms—share no matter what group they have made their target:[1]

- *Paranoia*. Hate sites promote the idea that conspiracies are everywhere. The target group is part of a conspiracy waged against good, honest people. The targets are blamed for economic and social problems. Those who set up the Web sites commonly invent evidence, misrepresent facts, and play on ignorance to prove their claims.

- *Righteousness*. One commentator calls this the "hand of God." Most hate sites try to convince readers that their position is moral, ordained by a higher power. They fill their pages with biblical references to give the appearance of holiness or righteousness.

- *The end is coming*. Hate sites play on people's fears. They predict impending doom—the hour of Armageddon, the end of the world, the collapse of civilization—blaming the target group, of course.

Keywords spring up often, such as "white power," "revolution," "skinheads," "KKK" (the white supremacist group called the Ku Klux Klan). Less obvious words such as "conspiracy," "militia," "nationalism," and "activism" can also be tip-offs, especially when combined with other signs. "Revisionism" is the term used by Holocaust deniers to describe their belief that millions of Jews were not killed by German Nazis during World War II—a complete denial of this major and tragic period of European history. Several humanitarian organizations actively keep track of hate groups and their efforts.

Cults, on the other hand, try to lure converts to their fanatical beliefs, and they usually want newcomers to join up—sometimes resulting in illness, deprivation, and death. A few signs include requests for surrender of self and a big financial commitment. Cults usually promise a future filled with a new level of joy or excitement that will carry members away from the boredom of this world. They are also usually headed by a single, dynamic prophet—the one true prophet of truth. And converts are usually enticed to join them in residence.[2] A cult can be powerfully attractive and seem to provide a safe home where all decisions are made for its members, but their fanaticism leaves no room for freedom, growth, and choice.

As CNET reporter Keith Ferrell once put it, "As with the real world, the virtual world calls for preparedness, alertness, armor."[3]

5

An Internet Lie Detection Kit

Maybe what we really need is a sort of Internet lie detector—a way to separate what is true from what is not. Common sense is the most effective weapon against being taken in. Robert A. Steiner, an expert on fraud and scams, gives seminars to police officers on detecting hoaxes. His advice for everyone is this: Just ask yourself, "Does it make sense?" He suggests taking time to think about what is being sold—or about what someone is trying to persuade listeners to believe. One's own common sense is the best defense.[1]

In this chapter, using common sense—

and a few other defense techniques as well—to detect Internet hoaxes will be explored.

When in Doubt, Ask Questions

How can anyone sort out what is real and what is fiction? To expand on the discussion in the previous chapter about knowing your sources, here are some more key questions to ask when evaluating a Web site.

Does the site give the date when it was last revised? This may seem like a minor point, but when checking on a topic that may change in response to new research or events, it may not make sense to spend any time at all reading material that was written several years ago. Time-sensitive information may be out of date. An old Web page for a space exploration program may not have been updated after the spacecraft launch in 1998. So, this Web site will not give up-to-date information about what has happened to the spacecraft since. Even if the Web site does not contain information that may be out of date, if the author has not returned to it for several years, this may indicate a lack of interest in its accuracy or thoughtful presentation in the first place.

Is this the latest news on this topic? For breaking news, is there a follow-up story? A story appeared recently in all the online newspapers about pools of water detected on the surface of Mars. NASA called a news conference to set the story right. True, scientists had discovered new and convincing signs of water in a lot of photographs taken by the Mars

When Internet news sources got the facts wrong about the images from the Mars Global Surveyor, NASA had to call a special news conference to clear up the confusion.

Global Surveyor spacecraft, but that is not the same as seeing the waters of Lake Superior lapping the shores. But anyone who read the first stories and did not read the follow-up could easily miss the corrected news.

Once again, who is the author, what are the author's credentials, and what objectives does the author have? To sell something? To express enthusiasm (for example as a fan club member would)? To promote a point of view? To educate?

Is the material presented as fact or is it frankly stated that it is opinion? (If it claims to be fact, do not just assume that it is, though. Be ready to use critical thinking to examine the claim carefully.)

What assumptions does the author make? What assumptions are you making? Examine each statement. Is every part of it supported with evidence? If not, the author may not really have the facts pinned down. Or do you know that it is true on your own? If solid support is not in the writing or in your own experience, and you believe the statements, then you are making some assumptions. Of course, everyone operates on some assumptions, or hunches, but the better they are supported with fact, the more accurate the assumptions will be.

Is the writing clear or ambiguous? Is there more than one way to interpret the writing? If so, the writer may not have thought the ideas through very carefully. Or the writer may be intentionally creating smoke screens to confuse readers and fool them. For example, one psychic predicted that "the Pope will become ill and could die." Many people would assume that she was asserting that the Pope would suffer a serious illness close to death. In fact, she worded her prediction so that even if the Pope only had the sniffles but was otherwise in excellent health throughout the year, she still would claim her prediction was correct. (She never said he *would* die, or even would be gravely ill. Yet many readers would assume that she would not bother to predict a cold.)

What evidence does the author provide? What kind of research methods did he or she use?

What is the level of detail offered? Is the coverage of the topic careful and thorough? Thrown together and argumentative? Can the information be verified somewhere else? What evidence is offered for statements made?

What organization or group sponsors the site? What can be found out about the organization? Does it have a biased point of view? Does another site back up the information without having the same special motives, such as trying to sell a product or service or idea?

What do the Web site's graphics tell about its intention? An emphasis on graphics, animation, and fun may indicate a less careful, accurate approach to facts. When looking for dependable information, really jazzy graphics may be a sign to proceed at one's own risk. Use critical thinking skills to evaluate for yourself, though—because even serious researchers can enjoy creating graphics and making a Web page inviting. And no one ever said good information had to be boring.

Persuasive Techniques Are Everywhere

Propaganda is just a set of techniques for persuading through manipulation—and in milder form it is all around us. Marketing and advertising executives make use of persuasive methods to sell products and build positive images for businesses. Politicians try to earn votes by smiling, agreeing with everyone, and cooing at babies. Even charities, such as the United Way, and religious leaders use sales or persuasive techniques to convince people to contribute to a cause. Occasionally, so do teachers and parents—and kids. (Ever try persuading your parents by pleading, "Aw, please, all the kids are doing it"? That is a classic persuasive technique called "The Bandwagon." It is also an emotional appeal.) Anyone who wants to persuade other people of a point of view, attitude, or belief will very likely use some of these techniques at one time or another.

The important point for everyone to remember is to be aware of the techniques. Watch for the sales pitch and understand how it works. Once the persuasive edge is recognized, it is disarmed. It no longer has the same power, and it is easier to make objective decisions and avoid being manipulated unfairly. It is important to be able to tell the difference between straight information or educational material and a clear attempt to persuade.

The use of persuasive terms and approaches does not make anyone a "bad guy" automatically. However, persuasive techniques do make use of tricks and sleight of hand. On the Web and in everyday life, it is important to know when these techniques are being used. Here are a few to keep in mind:

- Bandwagon—persuading people to do something by letting them know that other people are doing it. Humans are social, and they like to be part of the group. Knowing that other people believe something or have agreed to something makes it sound like a good thing to believe or do. In school, someone might say, "All the kids are doing it." A Web page for a diet aid might claim, "More dieters use 'KwikLoss' than any other brand." However, without more information, the reader does not know where KwikLoss obtained that "fact." (From an independent survey? Or from the company's own database? Or maybe the advertising manager just thought the statement sounded good.) It definitely would be a good idea to know more about the product than that before using it.

- Appeal to authority, or testimonial—using a figure of authority or famous person to recommend or endorse a belief or activity. For example, an Olympic star's picture appears on a Web page for "BreakfastYummies" cereal. (The implied message: You, too, can be an Olympic star, if you start your day with . . . BreakfastYummies!)

- Repetition—saying a motto, slogan, or brand name over and over until it sticks in people's

DANGERSLIM

The Latest Diet Pills You'll Be Dying to Use!

Tired of exercising daily in an effort to lose your unwanted pounds? *Dangerslim* is the product for you. Need to lose weight quickly and safely in a short amount of time? Try *Dangerslim*. **LOSE 10 POUNDS OR MORE IN A WEEK!**

Fat Melts Away

When you take a *Dangerslim* pill, you'll feel the fat melting off you instantly. Not in a day, not in 6 hours, not even in 45 minutes—**INSTANTLY!**

Exercising and dieting take too long, but you will see the effects of *Dangerslim* right away. **BE THE SIZE YOU WANT TO BE**, without the exercise!

Lose Weight Safely

In our extensive laboratory studies* on the effects of *Dangerslim*, we've proven that *Dangerslim* is safe for most people.

IT'S TIME TO GET SLIM. Call now to order, and if you are not completely satisfied with our product, we'll send you a second order at a **DISCOUNTED PRICE** within ninety days.

Ask yourself this: Are you sick of sweating for hours under the hot lights of the gym? If so, then *Dangerslim* is the product for you! We'll help you **LOSE WEIGHT QUICKLY** with just one simple pill. What are you waiting for? Get to the phone now and order *Dangerslim*!

Eat All You Want . . . And Still Lose Weight!

*Studies done only on lab mice.

Advertising is meant to entice customers. But what is said about a product, or the effect of the product, is not necessarily true. A savvy surfer uses clues to sort truth from fiction.

minds as right, or true, or just plain memorable. Many advertisers use a rule of thumb: Repeat the product name at least four times in a commercial. It is an effective trick, and a Web page that mentions the product many times hammers home the brand name (or basic concept, or hate slogan—depending on the writer's purpose).

• Emotional words—using emotion to sway even the most careful thinker. Someone may use any of a wide range of emotions, such as fear (one of the most powerful), sentimentality, patriotism, sense of family, loyalty, and pride. This trick is so powerful that it deserves a place among the prime examples of unclear thinking known as fallacies. (A fallacy is a statement or argument based on false or invalid reasoning. "Appeal to emotion" is a fallacy if it is used in place of logical reasoning, since an argument is not made true just because we are fearful, proud, or love our country.)

False Logic

In addition to these basic persuasive techniques, nearly fifty other common fallacies creep into arguments and persuasive discussions. Sometimes writers and speakers rely on these fallacies innocently, without realizing what they are doing. Often, though, they do use false reasoning on purpose, hoping to fool readers and listeners into looking at a topic a certain way. In either case, truth and accuracy get lost in the shuffle. Here are just a few of the most common of these blocks to clear thinking and honest discussion.

- Personal attack (also known by its Latin name, *ad hominem*)—attacks the person putting forth an idea. For example, "Look at the candidate's stupid yellow tie. Would you want a state governor who would wear such dorky clothes?" This fashion critique might have a place at a fashion show, but what does it have to do with a candidate's qualifications for office?

- Flattery—always a good way to distract a listener's attention from the soundness of an argument. An e-mail sales pitch might begin with something like this: "Because you have shown your discerning taste in music in the past, we are sure you will appreciate the new CD just out from Les Belles Dames. Click here . . ."

- Begging the question (circular reasoning)— The argument circles around and restates the premise without proving it. The premise may actually be true, but the speaker or writer has not proved it. For example: Objects that are not as dense as water float because these objects will not sink in water. (But of course an object that floats does not sink. The two parts of the statement say the same thing and the sentence never explains why.)

- Red herring—distracts attention with a completely unrelated comment. Red herrings often carry some emotional baggage to draw the reader in. For example, a personal Web site discussing health issues might throw in a completely unrelated remark about a political candidate. Readers who agree with the political remark will tend to transfer that agreement to the rest of the page's remarks. (The author apparently thinks most of his readers will agree.)

- Straw man—a sleight of hand that makes the speaker's position appear strong by portraying the opposition as weaker than it really is (setting up an opposition made of straw and then knocking it down). For example, a newsgroup writer might contend: "Senator Jones thinks we should spend less on health care for the elderly. Apparently she thinks she will never grow old, so we don't need to provide aid for anyone over sixty-five."

Many of these fallacies are like a magician's tricks. They use sleight of hand either to distract the listener's or reader's attention and then draw an unwarranted conclusion. Or they substitute something that appears to be the real thing but is not—something counterfeit. You can practice the art of catching fallacies by reading any magazine or newspaper, but the Internet can be a great place to hone this useful skill.[2]

Pseudoscientific Hoaxes

One of the strangest offshoots of the age of science in the twenty-first-century is the strength recently gained by an approach known generally as *pseudo-science*. Pseudoscience claims to be a science but uses non-scientific methods. The Internet is full of pseudoscientific Web sites, and many of them are difficult to differentiate from truly scientific sites.

What is the difference? Scientists are interested in building knowledge they can support with evidence gathered through careful observation. Their work is subject to review by other scientists who have the same commitment to experimentation and observation. The work of a scientist must be repeatable by other scientists who are able to obtain the same results by the same methods.

Pseudoscientists generally do not have the same commitment to supporting premises with carefully collected evidence. In their book *Science and Unreason*, Daisie Radner and Michael Radner propose several "marks" of a pseudoscientist—giveaway signals of a crank. What follows here is only a partial list. The presence of any of these signs in someone's work is a clear indication of pseudoscience. According to Radner and Radner, no one whose work contains any of these marks can be considered a true scientist. (They add that one cannot, however, assume that real science is being done just because none of these marks of a crank are visible.)

One can be sure, though, that if a Web page embraces *out-of-date thinking*—for example, the idea that the Earth is flat—the site is not scientific. Scientists are by profession thorough. If they have left a theory and gone on, they had good reasons and sound evidence. "Once a theory has been rejected," Radner and Radner explain, "scientists do not go back and take it up again unless they see how to make it work where it did not work before." Something has to have changed in the meantime to make going back worthwhile.[3]

Another mark of pseudoscience is a *grab-bag approach to evidence*—happily accepting large quantities of mediocre evidence as convincing proof. Quantity, not quality, is important to them. Scientists are fussier than that. They look for repeated confirmation by solid evidence that a premise is true. They also look for several different kinds of confirmations. Competing hypotheses have to offer less convincing evidence, or, preferably, should be disproved. A new hypothesis should also be capable of predicting new confirming evidence.

Pseudoscientists also delight in *hypotheses that cannot be proved or disproved*. However, a scientific theory must, by definition, be refutable—capable of being proven wrong. So, when a Web site puts forth a hypothesis that cannot be disproved, you know you have entered the land of pseudoscience, where anything is possible, nothing is impossible, and where you cannot be sure that anything is true—or even that it represents the best and soundest knowledge of our time.[4]

So, now take a look at a couple of kinds of hoaxes found on the Internet.

Medical Hoaxes, Advice, and Quackery

The Internet is a wonderfully freewheeling, hang-loose sort of place, and partly as a result, a great deal of what passes for medical information and advice whirs through cyberspace and finds its way onto people's computer screens. Credible information does exist, but so does a wide spectrum of questionable sources ranging from "snake-oil salesmen" and quacks to well-meaning individuals who just do not have their information right. Sound sources may include:

- government agencies

- academic institutions

- watchdog organizations

- professional medical associations

- research foundations

- major national disease-specific organizations, such as the American Heart Association

Less altruistic and objective sources include:

- managed care organizations (HMOs)

- hospital systems

- pharmaceutical or medical device manufacturers

- consulting firms

Once again, a healthy dose of skeptical judgment will help prevent swallowing nonsense whole or taking bad medical advice. Copy-cat sites often use names that sound like names of trusted medical resources. For example, the American College for Advancement in Medicine promotes chelation therapy for heart disease, a treatment about which the American Heart Association has stated, "We found no scientific evidence to demonstrate any benefit from this form of therapy."[5]

Recognizing a copy-cat site may not be easy. The best approach is to check the information you find on several sites (the Rule of Three again). However, it is important not to work from sites that are linked together. Working from a list of sites recommended by librarians is a good way to start. And watch for the red flags that are common on sites with an agenda. Using these guidelines will help in the search for objective, verifiable information.

Newsgroups often offer support groups that focus on particular ailments, but taking medical advice from newsgroup participants is a lot like walking into a room full of strangers and asking them whether they think cigarette smoking is harmful or whether safe sex is important. What credentials do they have? The newsgroup moderator does not control who gives advice and what qualifications they have. For example, a woman wrote in to a newsgroup that offers support to people with a genetic risk for abnormal blood-clotting (which may cause strokes). Its members share the same medical problem, but may or may not have a lot of knowledge about their condition or related problems. Seeking advice, the woman wrote that her grandmother was in the hospital with a stroke, and possibly a pulmonary embolism. She said that no intravenous blood thinning therapy had yet been prescribed. With only this information, other newsgroup members offered advice—based on little medical knowledge and very sketchy details about the grandmother's history and physical condition. Even a medical doctor's extensive training would not prepare her to make offhanded judgments in this case with so few details.

Misleading or quack medical sites often have their own brand of "red flags." Beware of a site that claims one medicine can cure an impossibly long list of unrelated diseases. If it seems impossibly long, it probably is. Talk of "new paradigms" and attacks on conventional medicine also may indicate the author prefers the unproved paths of pseudoscience to the more difficult but tested ways of medical science. Medicine is a practical science—that is, like technologists, its practitioners base their practice on what has been proved to work.

So, getting a second opinion is always good advice, along with a good dose of critical thinking. In addition, it is good to remember that the Internet can provide a wealth of information and psychological support—but it does not take the place of a well-trained and experienced medical care provider.

Virus Hoaxes

Everyone who uses the Internet knows how devastating a computer virus can be. It can wipe out everything on a hard drive. It can play havoc with programs and information filed away. Homework assignments can be destroyed. Years of correspondence by e-mail can get wiped out. So, one of the

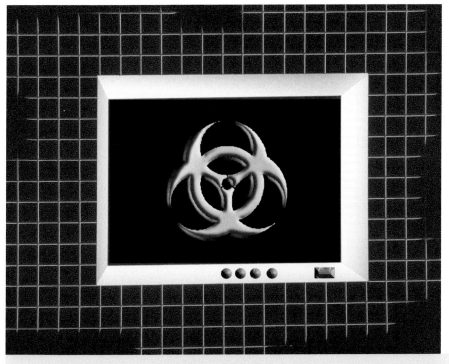

Viruses can be devastating. They can wipe out an entire hard drive in one click of an e-mail. Luckily, virus hoaxes can be easy to spot.

saddest of hoaxes is the virus hoax. But, just as watchful users can spot other kinds of hoaxes, fallacies, and bogus stories, they can catch a virus hoax in mid-sentence, as well.

Virus hoaxes are usually passed on in e-mail chain letters, in the same way the flesh-eating bananas hoax was passed on. The e-mails warn about a virus that does not exist—but the warnings themselves clog up the Internet if enough people respond to the usual urgent message to "pass this on to everyone you know." With hundreds of millions of people online, each one sending an average of six e-mails a day on an average day, it is mind-boggling to think how many e-mails would result if each one actually did send an e-mail warning to everyone he or she knows.

Experts at one company that creates anti-virus software put together this list of common phrases that turn up in virus hoax e-mails. The list actually outlines the content of most e-mail virus hoaxes.

> "If you receive an e-mail titled [name of e-mail virus hoax here], do not open it!" Sometimes there may be several exclamation points. Or it may say "with [name of e-mail virus hoax here] in the subject," or contain other slight variations.

> "Delete it immediately!" The writer will often warn to delete the message immediately without opening it.

> "It contains the [hoax name] virus." The e-mail will usually name a supposed virus.

"It will delete everything on your hard drive and . . ." The e-mail usually finishes this sentence with some extreme danger that is very unlikely to happen.

"This virus was announced today by [reputable organization name here]." The e-mail may try to reinforce its believability by appealing to authority—naming a source that people will respect. However, anyone can send an e-mail stating that a respected organization made an announcement—as we have already seen, e-mails can be untrue.

"Forward this warning to everyone you know!"[6]

6

Virtual Friends:
Chats or Cheats?

Chat rooms, IRC (Internet Relay Chat), Instant Messaging, and newsgroups can be both fun and informative. A teenager living on a farm in central Ontario, Canada, can "talk" through written messages with teenagers on other faraway farms or compare experiences with residents in cities and towns where she might never visit. A boy in San Francisco, California, can compare his baseball card collection to one belonging to an Internet user in Kansas. A mother at home with small children in upstate New York can share child-raising experiences, gardening tips, or recipes with an elderly man caring for his grandchildren in Austin, Texas. Eyewitness accounts of world events can be posted by individuals for everyone to read and discuss. This realm of the Net provides an exciting, open exchange of ideas, feelings, and information.

Talking in a chat room is like being in a room full of people—people you cannot see and almost always have never met. The conversation happens in "real time," that is, exchanges take place almost as if everyone really were in a room together.

Newsgroup discussions are not "real time"—that is, Janeen writes her question and posts it, and Eric, Alicia, and Amber may write replies that are also posted and read by Janeen and anyone else in the world (usually) who wants to. Newsgroup exchanges are often stored on a computer and made available to other Internet users for years—so it is a good idea to write carefully. Anything written for a newsgroup may be around a long time, stored somewhere in a computer on the Net, to be retrieved on purpose or by accident. Sometimes offhand comments made today can be pretty embarrassing when they turn up years later.

IRC or instant messaging require specialized software. IRC can enable any IRC user to buzz any other IRC user anytime they are both on their computers. Written conversations fly back and forth in real time, and when a user is "on the channel," whether he participates or not, his screen name appears automatically on a list available to everyone talking. With newsgroups, it is impossible to know who is paying

The Internet can be a wonderful place to chat with people about all kinds of things—but it can also be dangerous, since people can pretend to be anyone they want, knowledgeable or not, aboveboard or criminal.

attention as long as those "listening" do not write any comments. With IRC, though, everyone participating knows who is there. IRC has been around since about 1988 and has regularly been used since to relay first-person accounts of major world events, such as the Gulf War, the bombing of Serbia, and the World Cup. However, it is also used to discuss many other kinds of topics.[1]

With instant-messaging or chat-relay software, the user can also have more control over who joins the conversation. Private, unmonitored conversations between two people can take place, so this method of communication can require special caution if you do not know the other party. It works a lot like e-mail, but messages pop up on the screen when someone "calls." Then the conversation continues in real time.

Chat rooms and newsgroups are generally monitored by operators or moderators, who generally enforce basic rules of etiquette. Each individual newsgroup or chat room has its own moderator or operator, assigned by the sponsoring organization or company. Each one also has its own rules. Most forums require registration of some kind, or membership, and a member who breaks the rules can be barred from participating. Yet, here, too, a healthy dose of skepticism is a good antidote for trickery. People conversing in chat rooms, exchanging IRC comments, or writing messages in newsgroups are not always what they seem. People may not be who they pretend to be in any of these forums. Boys pretend to be girls, girls pretend to be boys, adults pretend to be kids, and kids pretend to be adults. Imagine how easy it would be for you to pretend to be somebody else in a chat room. That is how easy it is for everyone.

It may seem to be just harmless fun to pretend to be somebody that you are not in a chat room. But remember that other people may be playing the game, too, and their intentions may not be fun or harmless. They are invisible to you and you may think that you are invisible to them, but some people are very talented in learning important things about a person by asking questions. Recently, some commercial sites have begun to offer prizes for participating in marketing surveys, and then suddenly the innocent participant finds himself answering prying questions about shopping habits, family income levels, and other private information. Before he knows it, he has let his family in for a barrage of unwanted e-mails at the very least and—depending on the site's honesty—possibly much more annoying or dangerous intrusions. (See the guidelines at the end of this chapter for some ways to protect yourself and your family.)

Cause for Caution

The World Wide Web is just that—a worldwide network of diverse people of every description, both good and bad. Surfing the Net is a lot different from chatting with a longtime neighbor and/or a trusted family friend. People from all over the world have access to what is written in a newsgroup exchange.

Participants in chat rooms and newsgroups have to be members, but often nearly anyone in the world can become a member. On the Web—and especially in a chat room—people are on the honor system. Very little community pressure exists there to keep people from saying things they might otherwise be embarrassed about or ashamed of if they thought the truth would become public.

Stories that raise this caution turn up often in the news. One teenager, Katie Tarbox, wrote the story of her experience in a book, *Katie.Com*, published in 2000, when she was seventeen. She was thirteen when she met "Mark" in an AOL (America Online) chat room for teens. He said he was twenty-three. He was nicer to her than anyone she knew offline. She could not see him, but she saw pieces of evidence she liked. "I was impressed by the fact that he typed with proper punctuation and capitalized proper nouns and the first word of his sentences," she later explained. "Excellent grammar. A good vocabulary. I thought he must be all right."

When her swim team from New Canaan, Connecticut, traveled to a meet in Texas, Katie arranged to meet Mark in the hotel where she was staying as a member of the team. However, when she went to his hotel room, she discovered he was much older than he had said online—he was forty-one. She recounts that he pushed her up against a wall and began groping her almost as soon as she turned up at his hotel room.

This was definitely not the man of her dreams. "Mark was supposed to be better than this," she recounts in her book. "He was supposed to be patient and kind and generous. He was supposed to care about me."

Two years later, Katie Tarbox became the first person to successfully prosecute an Internet pedophile. Her attacker was president of an investment funds company in California, and he already had a history of preying on kids, according to the prosecutors. He was sentenced to eighteen months in jail in March 1998, after pleading guilty.

Katie Tarbox is a strong young woman, who reacted remarkably to a demoralizing and painful experience. She writes, " . . . as weird as it sounds, I had just lost my best friend"—a "friend" who was mostly a product of her own imagination and wishful thinking. She was also lucky, but she will probably always retain scars from the encounter. She has shared the experience in her book, and on her Web site, so others can take warning. She told *Seventeen* magazine writers in May 1999 that she wrote the book "because I didn't want anyone to have to suffer the way I did."[2]

Tarbox's experience is not isolated. A statewide undercover police effort in Wisconsin in February 2000 resulted in twenty-four arrests of adults preying on teenagers and children in Internet chat rooms. Sixteen of those arrested were nabbed after traveling to meet a teenager for a date made during computer conversations. Many were well-educated, prominent businessmen with families. One was said to be a priest. Another was a member of a popular singer's technical crew.[3]

There is nothing wrong with sharing ideas and thoughts—but sharing personal information online that can help identify you may be dangerous.

Safety Guidelines

So, a few basic rules make good sense when using Internet chat rooms and newsgroups or engaging in other Internet conversations:[4]

- Never give out personal information. Use only a screen name, not your real name.

- Never give anyone on the Internet your address, e-mail, or telephone number.

- Never arrange to meet anyone from a chat room in person at any time or any place. If someone persists in trying to make arrangements for you to meet them, tell your parents about it so that they can take appropriate action.

- Do not send personal photographs by mail or over the Internet to anyone you met on the Internet.

- Never give out information about any of your friends or family. Family income, address, personal health, credit card numbers, bank accounts, and shopping habits are just a few examples of the sort of information that should be kept private.

- If you suspect that someone is not who he or she is pretending to be, or if you feel that the conversation is getting too personal and is making you uncomfortable, get out of it. Break it off. If anything happens online that makes you uncomfortable, or if someone insists on bothering you even when you made it clear that you do not want to be bothered, let someone in authority know. Tell your parents and the operator of the chat room, newsgroup, or IRC channel.

The key phrases to remember are: "Keep your privacy" and "Have fun, but always remain skeptical." If you do, your experiences on the Internet can remain both rewarding and safe.

7

Cool Surfing!

The trick to not getting taken on the Internet is to surf, explore, and enjoy its diversity—while keeping cool. Before becoming either angry at, enchanted by, frightened by or "sold on" anything, keep these few guidelines in mind:

- Do not take what you see and read at face value.

- Know your sources.

- Watch for signs of unprofessionalism and unreliability.

- Watch for signs of bias.

- Ask questions and reserve judgment—while remaining ever skeptical.

- Always protect your own privacy and that of your family.

These guidelines are especially important if you are going to depend on any Internet information in the same way you might listen to your doctor or a teacher or a trusted friend. Find out as much as you

The trick to not getting taken on the Internet is to keep cool while you surf and explore.

can about a site. Use the most reliable sources you can. Then make decisions. When new and better information may come in, be ready to be flexible and change your judgment.

Most of all, remember the adage, "Doubt is the beginning of wisdom." But it is only the beginning. True wisdom comes from constantly sifting through everything and thinking about it—both on the Internet and in life. So . . . here's to cool surfing!

Appendix: About "Alien Abductions"

Since about the 1960s, many claims have been made of "alien abductions"—kidnapping of humans by extraterrestrial beings.[1] Could there really be space-ships from other worlds traveling in Earth's skies and kidnapping people? Even though some people do believe in UFOs (unidentified flying objects, or flying saucers), most scientists remain skeptical. Astronomers in particular—who spend most of their professional careers looking at the skies—are among the most skeptical. The problem is that just about all of the stories about UFOs are anecdotes.

There is no solid and unquestioned evidence that they actually exist aside from the stories people tell about them. As scientist Carl Sagan wrote in a *Parade* magazine article in 1995, "Everything hinges on the matter of evidence. On so important a question as UFOs, the evidence must be airtight. The more we want it to be true, the more careful we have to be. No witness say-so is good enough. People make mistakes. People play practical jokes. People stretch the truth for money, attention or fame. People occasionally misunderstand what they are seeing. People sometimes even see things that aren't there."[2]

Extraordinary claims require evidence that is

extraordinary. The idea that Earth is being visited (some say almost daily) by highly intelligent visitors from another planet is certainly an extraordinary claim. If it were true, it would be one of the most important discoveries in world history. And yet all the "evidence" we have amounts to unproven stories that people tell us and occasional fuzzy pictures or videotapes of objects in the skies that cannot be identified as anything other than fuzzy photographs and videotapes of "objects." They are truly UFOs— "Unidentified Flying Objects." While some people may see them as flying saucers from outer space, others may see them as paper plates tossed into the air and photographed in motion. Since paper plates are not such extraordinary objects and spacecraft from another world certainly are dramatically extraordinary, the burden falls upon those who claim that they are spacecraft to provide evidence that this is the case. So far, as noted by Carl Sagan, that evidence is sorely lacking.

Chapter Notes

Introduction

1. John R. Henderson, "ICYou See: A Guide to the World Wide Web, The ICYouSee Guide to Critical Thinking About What You See on the Web," June 13, 2000, <http://www.ithaca.edu/library/Training/hott.html> (July 3, 2000).

2. Ibid.

3. Clarence Darrow, a criminal defense lawyer who was famous for his tough and critical questions, wrote in his essay, *Why I Am An Agnostic*: "Skepticism and doubt lead to study and investigation, and investigation is the beginning of wisdom." Over time, this may have been shortened to "Doubt is the beginning of wisdom."

Chapter 1. The Great Flesh-Eating Banana Hoax

1. The San Fernando Valley Folklore Society's Urban Legends Reference Pages, March 1, 2000, <http://www.snopes.com> (July 6, 2000).

2. *Webster's College Dictionary* (New York: Random House, 1991), p. 637.

3. Jan Harold Brunvand, *Curses! Broiled Again!: The Hottest Urban Legends Going* (New York: W.W. Norton and Company, 1989), p. 11.

4. *Webster's*, p. 517.

5. Centers for Disease Control and Prevention, Media Relations Office of Communication Web site, January 28, 2000, <http://www.cdc.gov/od/oc/media/pressrel/r2k0128.htm> (June 18, 2000).

6. Google home page 2001, <http://www.google.com> (October 30, 2000).

Chapter 2. Looking for Answers on the Internet

1. Steve Lawrence and C. Lee Giles, "Accessibility and Distribution of Information on the Web," n.d., <http://www.metrics.com> (April 6, 2000).

2. Google home page 2001, <http://www.google.com> (July 4, 2000).

3. Lawrence, "Accessibility and Distribution of Information on the Web."

4. Ibid.

5. "Forget the Search Engines," by David Biro as told to Atul Gawande, surgical resident and staff writer for *The New Yorker*, June 14, 2000, <http://slate.msn.com> (June 17, 2000).

6. American Academy of Dermatology, n.d., <www.aad.org> (February 4, 2001).

7. John R. Henderson, John R., "ICYou See: T is for Thinking," June 13, 2000, <http://www.ithaca.edu/library/Training/hott.html> (July 3, 2000).

Chapter 4. Investigating the Sources

1. Based on Keith Ferrell, "The Dark Side of the Web—Hatemongers," July 10, 1997, <http://coverage.cnet.com/Content/Features/Dlife/Dark/ss02a.html> (July 4, 2000).

2. Ibid.

3. Ibid.

Chapter 5. An Internet Lie Detection Kit

1. Robert A. Steiner, *Don't Get Taken! Bunco and Bunkum Exposed* (El Cerrito, Calif.: Wide-Awake Books, 1989), p. 161.

2. Jerry Cederblom and David W. Paulsen, *Critical Reasoning: Understanding and Criticizing Arguments and Theories* (Belmont, Calif.: Wadsworth Publishing Co., 2000), pp. 85–86.

3. Daisie Radner and Michael Radner, *Science and Unreason* (Belmont, Calif.: Wadsworth Publishing Co., 1990), p. 29.

4. Ibid., pp. 17–42.

5. American Heart Association site, "Chelation Therapy," 2000, <http://www.americanheart.org/Heart_and_Stroke_A_Z_Guide/chelat.html> (July 4, 2000).

6. Symantec, Inc., April 4, 2000, <http://service1.symantec.com/SUPPORT/nav.nsf/docid/199904120913 1106&src=n> (April 4, 2000).

Chapter 6. Virtual Friends: Chats or Cheats?

1. Angus J. Kennedy, *The Internet: The Rough Guide 2000* (New York: Rough Guides Ltd., 1999), pp. 186–187.

2. <http://www.seventeen.com/entertainment_buzz/books.cfm?id=3491&page_id=1469>, ©1999 (July 4, 2000).

3. State of Wisconsin Department of Justice, February 18, 2000, <http://www.doj.state.wi.us/news/ 021800.htm> (July 4, 2000); February 20, 2000, <http://www.hotstreak.net/anti/news/feb00/200200a.htm> (July 4, 2000).

4. "KidsHealth for Parents," 2000, <http://kidshealth.org/parent/positive/family/net_safety_p8.html> (October 25, 2000).

Appendix. About Alien Abductions

1. William F. Williams, ed., *Encyclopedia of Pseudoscience from Alien Abductions to Zone Therapy* (New York: Facts On File, Inc., 2000), pp. 1–2.

2. Carl Sagan, "Crop Circles and Aliens: What's the Evidence?" *Parade* (*The Baltimore Sun*), December 3, 1995, pp. 10–12, 17.

Glossary

bias—Prejudice that blocks impartial judgment; one-sided view, often prompted by motivation to see things in a certain way.

bunco—Also known as "bunko"; a confidence game, or swindle, in which the swindler gains the unsuspecting person's confidence and then cheats the victim.

domain name—The unique name that defines an Internet site, designated by the first few parts (usually two or three) separated by periods; a domain name points to one specific machine.

fallacy—A statement or argument based on unsound reasoning.

fraud—A trick intended to deceive someone in order to gain unfairly or unlawfully.

hate—To advocate hostility or violence toward, lies about, or separation from a group of people.

hate site—A Web site that advocates hatred and hate crimes.

hoax—An act intended to deceive or trick.

hyperlink—Text that contains "links"—words or phrases the reader can click on to obtain additional information or comment from another document or from another place in the same document.

newsgroups—Discussion groups on Usenet, an international system with no centralization, which uses hundreds of machines to pass on comments; about ten thousand newsgroups exist, although only about half are available on the Internet.

paranoia—Extreme, unreasonable distrust of others.

propaganda—The systematic attempt to influence people through the use of symbols, including words, pictures, sounds, uniforms, and so on; propaganda can range from open attempts to persuade to less obvious methods, sometimes using unrelated means of pressuring opinions or behavior.

pseudoscience—A method, theory, or practice that claims to be scientific but is not.

righteousness—The quality of being without blame or guilt.

scam—A business scheme for cheating someone; a misrepresentation to fool a victim; a swindle.

search engine—A computer program on the Internet that indexes subjects covered on Web pages and allows users to search for coverage of specific topics.

tabloid—A newspaper in small format that gives stories in condensed form—usually having an overstated, sensational style and illustrated with gruesome photographs.

tilde—A symbol (~) used in some URLs, often indicating a Web site that has not registered its own domain name, and therefore possibly a site belonging to an individual.

typographical—Relating to the arrangement and appearance of words.

urban legend—An unverified, generally bizarre, but believable story delivered by word of mouth (including e-mail); today's folklore.

URL—"Uniform Resource Locator" or Web page address.

virus—A computer virus; that is, a program introduced into a computer system to cause mischief or harm to the workings of the computer.

Further Reading

Barksdale, Karl and J. Alan Baumgarten. *Exploring the Internet: Cyberspace Odyssey*. Cincinnati: South-Western Publishing Company, 1997.

Gralla, Preston. *Online Kids: A Young Surfer's Guide to Cyberspace*. New York: John Wiley & Sons, Inc., 1999.

Lawler, Jennifer. *Cyberdanger and Internet Safety: A Hot Issue*. Berkeley Heights, N.J.: Enslow Publishers, Inc., 2000.

Owen, Trevor, et al. *The Learning Highway: Smart Students and the Net, Revised*. Buffalo, N.Y.: Firefly Books, Ltd., 1998.

Ruchlis, Hy, with Sandra Oddo. *Clear Thinking: A Practical Introduction*. Foreword by Isaac Asimov. New York: Prometheus Books, 1990.

Schrecengost, Maity. *Researching Events*. Fort Atkinson, Wisc.: Highsmith Press, 1998.

Steiner, Robert A. *Don't Get Taken!: Bunco and Bunkum Exposed*. El Cerrito, Calif.: Wide-Awake Books, 1989.

Internet Addresses

Ask Jeeves for Kids

<http://www.ajkids.com>

> *Jeeves, the butler (based on a character created by the writer P. G. Wodehouse), accepts questions in plain English, and then takes the user to the appropriate site. Jeeves also offers lists of other search engines to use.*

IC You See: A Guide to the World Wide Web

<http://www.ithaca.edu/library/Training/ICYouSee.html>

> *Written in a breezy style, this site uses critical thinking strategies.*

KidsClick!

<http://Sunsite.berkeley.edu/KidsClick!>

> *This search site, developed by librarians, searches a list of prescreened sites. Users can look up keywords or use subject directories.*

Yahooligans

<http://www.yahooligans.com>

> *A search engine designed for kids ages seven to twelve, offering keyword searches and subject directories.*

Pseudoscience and Other Hoaxes

Committee for the Scientific Investigation of Claims of the Paranormal (CSICOP, pronounced "SY cop")

<http://www.csicop.org>

Encourages the critical investigation of paranormal and fringe-science claims from a scientific point of view and gives out factual information.

Urban Legends

The AFU & Urban Legends Archive

<http://www.urbanlegends.com>

An archive of urban legends.

The San Fernando Valley Folklore Society's Urban Legends Reference Pages

<http://www.snopes2.com>

Another archive of urban legends.

Hate Groups and Cults

Center for the Study of Hate and Extremism

<http://www.hatemonitor.org>

This Web site at California State University examines how bigotry and terrorism threaten human rights.

Media Awareness (Canada)
Challenging Online Hate

<http://www.media-awareness.ca/eng/issues/
internet/hintro.htm>

> *This Canadian Web site provides resources from police, government, community groups, and the Internet industry to help young people cope with hatred they find online. The site is committed to helping young people learn how to detect bias, recognize hate propaganda online and online hate recruitment, and protect their personal privacy online.*

On Medical Hoaxes and Fraud

Quackwatch

<http://www.quackwatch.com>

> *Operated by Stephen Barrett, M.D., this site contains articles about medical hoaxes, scams, and fraud. It provides clear, no nonsense information about popular cures and treatments. Questions related to consumer health are also answered by e-mail.*

The National Council Against Health Fraud

<http://www.ncahf.org>

> *Provides responsible, reliable, evidence-based information about consumer health issues, helping the consumer to tell the difference between what is and what is not sound.*

Index